WALKING HOME

GROWING UP HISPANIC IN HOUSTON

SARAH CORTEZ

Texas Review Press
Huntsville, Texas

FIRST EDITION, 2012
Requests for permission to reproduce material from this work should be sent to:

Permissions
Texas Review Press
English Department
Sam Houston State University
Huntsville, TX 77341-2146

Acknowledgements:

The following poems have appeared in these journals and anthologies:

A Student's Treasury of Texas Poetry, "Visiting" and "Surf Fishing"
Brazos River Review: "Question," "Pot of Rouge."
New Texas: "Charlie."
Red Boots and Attitude: An Eclectic Anthology Showcasing Contemporary Texas
    Women Writers: "Magic" and "Fish to Catch."
Riding Low on the Streets of Gold: Latino Literature for Young Adults: "Haunt,"
    "Walking Home."
SWIRL: "Haunt."
Texas Poetry Calendar 2008: "Seguin."
Texas Poetry Calendar 2009: "On South Main."
The Texas Review: "The Claiming," "Harmony Wedding Chapel," "Happiness."
TimeSlice: Houston Poetry 2005: "Delivery."
The Weight of Addition: "Seguin."

Grateful acknowledgment is given to the University of Houston's Center for Mexican American Studies for a visiting scholar position which enabled this book to be envisioned and written. Grateful acknowledgment is also given to the Virginia Center for the Creative Arts for a fellowship furthering the revision of this book.

Grateful acknowledgment is given to the Congregation of the Sisters of Charity of the Incarnate Word, Houston, Texas, for permission to feature the Annunciation Window, Villa de Matel Chapel, on the front cover.

Cover design by Nancy Parsons, Graphic Design Group

Library of Congress Cataloging-in-Publication Data

Cortez, Sarah.
  Walking home : growing up Hispanic in Houston / Sarah Cortez.
      p. cm.
  ISBN 978-1-933896-83-0 (pbk. : alk. paper)
  1. Cortez, Sarah. 2. Authors, American--21st century--Biography.
  3. Hispanic American women authors--Biography. I. Title.
  PS3553.O7227Z46 2012
  818'.603--dc23
  [B]
                                    2012010492

In memory of my parents,
Piedad María Talamántez Garza
and
Ignacio Pérez Cortez

CONTENTS

Walking Home—ix

Section One

Section Two

Walking Home

Step up to the large stained-glass window with me. For now, do not be anxious about its entire picture—who the people are, or why they are pierced and longing. Press your nose against the leaded glass. It will warm with your breath. Touch it.

Here, trapped in the hues and slivers, are the unlived dreams of my family—mother, father, me. Here, too, are captured the myths that held us secure. Their mystery swirls before us in unmentionable contours, stunned into the eternal placement of sacred tableaux. I will explain how the shapes and colors of glass chunks emanate meaning. They will reveal to you their unwritten power.

Come, take my hand. Look closely. Touch the cold.

SECTION ONE

White

The first color you will notice is a pure white surrounding the entire stained-glass window. Its small rectangles form a necklace of refracted sunlight. Unobtrusive and beautiful. This is the strong, pure color of my mother's lifelong dream for many children of her own. Her precious and unrealized dream frames her life, my life as her only daughter, and my father's life as her one and only husband of over fifty years. When she was a young girl, perhaps her dream went like this.

*   *   *

While ironing one afternoon in the front bedroom, my mother steps into her sweetest dream. This dream spins itself in a world far from this white, wood-framed farmhouse in the hot, sandy soil of Floresville, Texas. Far from the twice-daily milking of cows, near-dawn collecting of hens' eggs, and slopping the hogs. Far from this place made safe by the endless, hard work of her parents, a sister, her brothers, and herself.

My mother dreams children as black-headed as she. Dark-skinned, roly-poly babies to be swung and tickled. Slightly older babies experimenting on fat, brown legs—the miracle of walking. Children with pupils black as a starless night. She can see how her children, herself, and an unimaginable husband will pray the rosary every night—as is done in her parents' home. The oval kitchen table and chairs pulled back so everyone can kneel in a circle on worn linoleum.

My mother dreams of cooking every night for her large family—one child a year. She will roll out tortillas, the cast-iron griddle hot against the lard, flour, and milk—the fragrance of reward and dusk's home-coming.

She wonders which of her many children will be her favorite. In this household, she is the favorite of both her young mother and her older father. He has nicknamed her *Prietita* in honor of her skin—darker than the boys or the one sister. My mother almost always chooses to work in the house with her mother, even though her father prefers her help in the fields to that of her angular, strong, younger sister. In the orderly house she can dream of her future among the dark, wood furniture and white walls—a future of so many babies, so much warmth cuddling against her chest.

The sweat starts to bead on her forehead. There's not much breeze in Texas summers even in this room with the wide screened windows on two sides and the front door propped open. She doesn't mind the sweat of hard work—no one here on the farm does anything but work. It gives both routine and the meaning for routine. One day she will starch and iron for many children. Dresses with sashes for the girls. Shirts with collars for the boys. It's going to be a good future. She can feel it coming, the anticipation welling up from somewhere deep inside—too deep to even try to understand. She feels it in the irregular beating of her heart. A rhythm she will not understand until her deathbed. Its last visitation.

Sometimes when she is trying to sleep at night, this heart of hers jumps inside her thin chest. At those moments, she doesn't move. She doesn't ask her younger sister, Estellita, lying next to her for help, frowning even as she sleeps. No. She waits listening to the coyotes howl and the farm dogs bark in return. She concentrates on the familiar smell of the sand—always present inside the screen doors and windows. She comforts herself by repeating prayers in Spanish. Finally, sleep will take her—lips stopping in mid-word. Her nightgown will be soaked with sweat. She will not mention her odd, dancing heart—even to her beloved mother—in the morning.

Nimbus

Look at the halo of bright energy surrounding each person embedded in the stained glass. Emanating outward, glowing—it holds your gaze as the holy is ordained to do. Do not fear this manifestation of transcendent power. In this power is contained the promise of divine intervention called *miracle*.

My mother's mother asked for such a miracle. Perhaps, this is how it happened.

*   *   *

A young, dark-skinned woman—my mother—lies silent on white sheets. The delicacy of white-painted ironwork curls over her black hair, the strands separated by sweat. She is dying. The stooped doctor has left the farmhouse already; he doesn't need to stay for this.

My grandmother prays in the dusty hallway. She keeps the door to the front bedroom open in case her closest daughter cries out. The softness of Spanish entreats the gilt-framed picture of the Virgin Mary on the wall. She cannot relinquish her oldest daughter's soul. The worn and smooth, beige rosary beads slip past her fingers. Her older husband has retreated to the small foyer at the other end of the hallway running the length of the house. If either one of them looked up, the other would be there—anchoring the opposite and opposing axes of their farmhouse. But neither one will look at anything other than what is providing solace in this hushed time of dying. She gazes only at the Virgin; he smokes unfiltered Camels. Fingernails—black with the crushed blood of too many farming accidents—stub out the butts in a small, round glass ashtray in the center of a mock tractor wheel.

Incessantly the prayers rise from grandmother's heart. Her lips outpour syllable upon syllable, phrase after phrase. Each prayerful formula propelled by belief—a faith so intimate, so complete that finally the sky itself begins to rise with it. Outside, the oceanic blue wideness of Texas sky dislocates itself from the daily reality of munching cattle, peanut crops, and drying wells. Her faith has rent heaven. The immanent is deserted while the cresting wave caused by grandmother's inviolate faith breaks over and against the most precious Lady, His mother—the Virgin Mary. At this precise moment, the Virgin smiles at the praying mother on her knees on the ridged plastic runner in the hallway of the Garza farm outside Floresville, Texas.

Only for a second or less. Just a smile. Nothing else in the picture flickers. The Virgin's two hands stay poised framing her pierced heart and its corona of yellow roses. Her head doesn't nod. Her golden halo does not grow more or less intense. Yet, at the moment of the smile, my grandmother feels her own stricken heart ease. Her daughter, Piedad, will live. Death will not claim her today; the Blessed Virgin has smiled.

*　　*　　*

Inside the bedroom my mother stirs briefly, her head nestled on pillowcases edged with strong, blue lace crocheted by her mother listening to the radio at night with the entire family. She has felt the miracle without knowing the events in the hallway. The kidney infection has stopped its killing of her, will allow her slight body to begin recovering. She struggles to free her memory from the old doctor's sadness at her approaching death and his own lack of resources. She remembers what he discovered about her heart during the examination. She has a bad heart; she won't live past thirty or forty, at the most. She will die young. Younger than her mother is today. How can this be? Her father has already promised the reward of college to her, even though his sisters chide him for wanting to educate a girl. She's planning to be a teacher one day. Every night she studies by the kerosene lamp.

In the hallway her beloved mother—one devoted fist thumping her own chest—has already slipped into the prayers of thanksgiving for this blessing. This miracle.

My mother begins making plans.

Rose

Rose is the color of the inner womb. Each person whether male or female carries this potential place inside. It is the color of receptivity. The color of the place where we each make room for something new.

Its soothing aspect does not connote weakness but strength. Its closeness to pastel does not release it into the realm of the unrealized and vague. But rather, masks its nourishing stamina.

To create this color inside one's self takes more than most of us humans possess most of the time. It takes a widening of the heart into acceptance of the unknown and the uncontrollable. This is how I imagine my mother—Piedad Garza Cortez—thinking as I lay deep in her womb desperate to speed my arrival into this 1949 world.

*   *   *

My life exists only in what is in this room, in my belly, in our own small house. Doctor Brown has ordered me to stay in bed. We're trying to save the baby. Flat on my back in a pale pink nightgown and pink quilted bed jacket, I watch the shifting lengths of light across furniture. Once or twice a day I get up to pull the thick white cord that adjusts the Venetian blinds against the early springtime heat.

The neighborhood is quiet except for a few barking dogs who rile up when the postman walks by. Often I slip the heavy, faceted blue beads of a rosary into my fingers. Praying is the only thing that connects me to reassurance. Steadily, desperately, I pray. Our Blessed Lady must understand—she was a mother herself. Her picture from the farmhouse in Floresville gazes down at me. The perfect corona of open yellow roses circling her heart seems to tremble in the heat of her flaming love. Rosary after rosary I send to her, asking for her intercession, asking that this baby be born whole and healthy, asking for another miracle.

I don't know if I should be begging for a miracle beyond the one that has already been granted—getting pregnant after the doctor had said, "Never again." But surely, since the novenas I prayed to St. Anne, gentle patroness of motherhood, resulted in this second baby, it won't be snatched from me. Won't be taken so we have to find another tiny, white coffin.

*   *   *

Baby, sweet little baby. Don't come yet. It's too soon. You haven't lived inside of me long enough. Wait, baby. Wait. The doctor says you can't survive so many months premature. Be patient, baby.

*   *   *

Yesterday I tried to walk to the neighborhood grocery store. An easy walk. Before I reached the end of the block I could feel a thin trickle of blood—the hemorrhaging that might be the baby leaking out between my legs. I could barely walk home. Every particle of me wanted to stay paralyzed on the hot cement sidewalk to help the baby stay inside. Yet, a coarse thread seemed to vibrate urgent and painful inside of my fear. It wouldn't let me stand still. It forced me to walk home, to call Ernie to come home from work to drive me to the doctor.

*   *   *

Little Baby, we only have one chance for you to live. Don't leave me like the first baby. Stay put. Let Ernie and I give you a home. Everything is ready for you, baby. You'll be fat and healthy. Just wait, baby, at least two more months. I promise I won't walk anymore until you're here. Don't become the hot trickle down my leg. I'll stay in this bed. Flat on my back. Praying.

Cobalt Blue

Touch this beautiful blue glass to feel its color. This is both the color created by sheer determination and the color that exists as a refuge when will fails. This color is the deepest of all the colors because it is built by the force of human resolve.

Think of it as the will to stay alive. It is what exists when Death circles. You will see it in the votive candles of old churches. Friend to flame, it protects the nimbus of white heat from the breath of the killing wind.

Its vigil is eternal; its friendship endless. It is the color my mother remembers every night as she un-dreams her own mother's death.

*   *   *

This will not happen. The drive into town for the week's groceries. Mom dressed up with purse, dark gloves, a matching hat. There will be no groceries. No need for food.

There will be no walking from the store knowing that the boy will carry the bags easily as he does every other week for the farmers' small change. No walking out of the store—Mother and Dad together. Him at her side hearing the odd, faint rush of air out of her lips. There will be no air. She will not ask to sit down for a small rest in the painted metal summer chairs outside of the grocery store. She will not sit down, her hand heavy on his arm. Too heavy. She will not close her eyes, the grey crown of long twisted braids around her head making her a queen. There will be no closing of her eyes. No eyelids. No eyes.

*   *   *

At the funeral home I will not watch my youngest brother disintegrate. His handsomeness always a curse. He will not denounce God because our mother is dead. There will be no death. His dark head will not bend into his sobs between heaving shoulders in a tight, blue dress suit.

I will not watch bent and sad friends of my mother limp out to the small cistern in the funeral home's patio to drink water out of the aluminum cup on a chain. There will be no water. No thirst. No chairs that rattle each time against the metal stand and metal drinking cup. There will not be an open patio adjacent to her coffin.

There will not be huge walls of flowers next to where she lies. I will not have to listen politely and with a broken heart to so many stories of her kindness to others, her generosity, her good works in the small town. No, there will be no translucent petals of pink and gold gladiolas rearing up like stallions in the niches inside the funeral home.

There can't be any candles. No candle holders. No, not the ones of cobalt blue glass in narrow, tall cylinders. I won't watch people struggle to light the charred wicks deep inside the blue recess of each candle with a safety match, then kneel to pray in front of mother's coffin.

No, mother's death will not happen. Didn't happen. Can't happen. Her heart will not fail. Just as mine will not fail. I have my own daughter now and the old doctor's prophecy about my heart giving out will not come true. I did not die before I reached forty, as he said. Surely, I can make it for a few more years. I will not leave my young daughter alone in the world. She needs more time to grow independent and become able to get along without me. She's not ready yet. I will not leave her alone.

I will not.

The Lady

See the Lady. A white mantle drapes her head framing smooth, pale cheeks and a warm smile. Her serene eyes have stared at sights you're not sure exist—God Himself, archangels, maybe, even the soul. She is comfortable with miracle and still believes in the infinite possibility of goodness on earth. She has many names, Pillar of Grace, Seat of Ivory, the Immaculate Virgin Mary, the Mother of God.

Up there in the prison of glass she is trapped and allows herself to be. Her heart is big enough to hold all the broken hopes and confusion of the human world. She opens herself up to whoever prays to her, for everyone responds differently in the face of her love.

When I see the Lady, I remember my father's early loss of his own beloved mother in the South Texas fishing town of Matagorda, Texas. The life-long trap of unsaid goodbyes and never-delivered hellos. He might tell of her death in this way.

*   *   *

Inside my eyelids I often see my mother's brief smile against the darkness—her thin lips a pink curve uplifted into pale cheeks. Her light blue eyes looking at me. This is where I go to see her now because she is no longer with us.

The journey begins in this way.

*   *   *

It is nighttime but Betty and I are not at our

house. We are at grandfather and grandmother's house. Betty, my oldest sister, and I are sick in bed. We have been put together in a single room, away from everyone else. All day long we have seen mother walking back and forth in the hallway.

Everyone here is sick—father, both grandparents, us. Only mother is well. Back and forth in the hallway, her steps unravel the pain in my head and body. Sometimes when I can force my eyes open, I see her worried face over our bed. Because of her belly—the new baby to come—she can't bend over too much. She talks to us, reaching one hand to touch each forehead. Then, I hear and feel her footsteps leave the small room.

How many days is it the same? Her light footsteps, my throbbing head, Betty coughing beside me. My own coughing sounding distant to my ears.

That was the beginning.

*   *   *

I slept badly, although I liked this house of grandfather's and grandmother's with its many small panes of glass for windows. Outside, the tall poles for drying his nets. The room was too small for all my questions. Why wasn't grandfather stomping around on the wood floors or out in the yard tending to his nets before the next fishing trip? Why was my own father sick and coughing in another room? Where were the rest of our brothers and sisters? Who was taking care of Wally, the baby?

Never had I been to grandmother's when she

didn't fix black coffee in the mornings. Where was she? There was only my mother to take care of all of us who were sick.

Later, Betty said she saw mother leave. I must've been asleep. Betty said mother was covered with a white sheet on a small bed. It must've been neighbors who carried the whole bed out into the cold. All the grown men in our family were still too sick to stand. We kids didn't know what it meant. Why would mother leave lying down?

No one asked us what we were thinking. No one said "dead" or "death." No one said "influenza."

*   *   *

One day I will find my mother again. I know this. The smile I carry inside of me will start to feel warm instead of damp and cold. Soon after her lips will become tinged with a slight color and become rounded. Her cheeks will stop looking drawn and tight.

The hard arc of her smile will loosen into words. "*Ven. Ven para 'ca.*" The long slender fingers of one hand will pat her white skirt. I will feel all the love inside of her asking me—yes, me—to come to her. To be at her side. She'll know how all of us kids have missed her. How our lives changed forever once she left. The step-mother with sharp Spanish from Mexico. The parceling out of even me—the eldest son—to relatives.

Each detail of her braided dark hair, of her long dress, of her leather shoes with tiny buttons will be calling to me, "*Ven. Ven. Ven, Ignacio.*" I can feel my decades of silent waiting for the touch of her fingers in my black hair. She will see how we still have the same color eyes.

She will no longer be inside of me. She will have stepped outside of the place I have carried her for so many years. By this stepping forth, she means for me to join her. It is time. Even though I sense the thickness of air separating us, I must go to her. She is calling. Finally, I hear her voice again.

The empty waiting is done. I step forward and end both our journeys.

The Son

Notice the lap of the Lady. There is a small boy on it. He's dressed in a white nightgown. He still gets afraid in the dark and doesn't like to sleep away from his parents.

He is lifting one small foot while his mother holds his hands for balance. The underside of his foot shows us a pink innocence unacquainted with roads, stiff leather, or sharp pebbles.

His father loves this small son of his. He considers this child of his to be perfect simply because he is the son, the father's gift to eternity.

While he works during the day, the father daydreams about what he and his son will do together one day. Maybe his son will learn his only trade; maybe they will work together in the heat of the day.

One son was born to my parents, only to die within three days of a rare birth defect. This happened two years before I was born. Even though my father never mentioned his loss and treated me as precious and wanted, I believe my father dreamed a son. Here is his dream.

*　　*　　*

A man's destiny is to have a son. It is part of God's great plan. The son carries the father's name, the father's blood. The son learns from the father. Slowly at first, the son is educated by his father. This is a father's duty and he takes pride in doing it well. Everything a father has learned about life, he will try to give to his son.

First, the son learns about the inside of

the home. The rules for helping mother, about respect and truth. How to pray. About "please" and "thank you." Then the son starts learning in the yard, in the garage. I will teach my son those things men know—how to saw, hammer, mow. How to prepare the wood before painting. How to run a fence so that it is straight and even. How to fix things. We will work outside together. Afterwards we will come inside the cool of the kitchen to drink from the pitcher of iced water sitting on the gray tile counter top. The small towels worn on the backs of our necks for sweat will feel like sudden ice.

During the winter months, I'll take him hunting for ducks and geese. We'll pack everything the night before except the bagged lunch Mom will put in the fridge. My son will be very sleepy—not used to getting up at four-thirty in the morning. I'll drive and he'll sit silent eating the egg sandwich Mom fried up last night. His without black pepper; mine covered in it. The slow chewing will keep him awake in the darkness of two-lane roads outside the city.

Once we arrive, I'll carry the big burlap sacks full of decoys through the mud and withered weeds to the pond. He'll be tall enough—just barely—to carry his own gun, barrel pointed to the ground as I've taught him. We won't complain, although both our sets of teeth will be chattering from the damp cold at such an early hour. Toes already numb in the heavy boots.

Around dawn we'll be settled in the blind. Decoys set. I'll look around at the creeping pink of sunrise. The mist will still be huddled against the grey water and the stalks of last summer's weeds. There will be no wind; no motion. I'll feel the weight of my waders outside the thick hunting pants. My son will be more fully awake now. The bill of his camouflage cap will rest low on his eyebrows. We'll both know that sitting silent, waiting for the birds to fly over so we can call them down, is as peaceful as life gets. That this waiting, this sure knowledge of good to come—the sharp kick of recoil against right shoulder, a hot dinner tonight of freshly killed birds—is perfect. That all of this has more of life's unpredictability, loss, and reward than anything in the city.

He'll smile again. I'll ask him, "Cold, son?" He'll square his thin shoulders and say, "No, sir." But I'll know he's a bit colder than he'd like to be—as I am. I'll say, "Listen for the birds. They'll start flying soon." He'll smile back at me, then let his face go serious.

Maybe he'll remember when he was younger and I used to take him outside on early fall nights to hear the geese calling as they flew south in their mysterious Vees. I'd hold him up in my arms and we'd both listen, hearing the rapidly disappearing honking of the big birds from so far away. Both feeling the urge to fly along in the wide-open sky, high and free. Powerful wings beating against cold air.

We'll settle in for the hunt together, both making sure our guns are handy. Shoulders hunched, breath a small white fog.

My son. My pride and joy.

Emerald Green

A green trellis weaves around these figures in the stained glass window we are studying. The deepness of color promises cool nourishment and endless bounty. Green's essence is hope. An undying look toward all horizons for good to arrive. Some might call the good to come "riches" or "good fortune." In my first memory, I knew it was "love" and I named it "mother."

*   *   *

A thin, cool sheet on the mattress. Four walls of crib in a pleasant, light-brown color. A bedroom. Dark pink on the walls and filtered light coming in tall, thin windows through white slats of Venetian blinds. In the kitchen—a room far away from my crib—sounds float to me. A mixmaster. The inexhaustible motor of my mother's mixer. Good things to eat will come later—that is what the motor's twirl means.

Now my concentration is fixed on the wood of my crib. The headboard goes straight up and at my feet the same block exists. But on the sides are only vertical bars. Between the light—freedom. Possibility. I desperately want to be outside this childish bed. Closer to the translucent, white net curtains framing each side window of this room. Closer to the good news called "mother." In her sturdy, strong arms, my lips pressed in her curled black hair. She doesn't know and wouldn't understand my urge to transgress structure, to leap over any boundary. To claim adventure for my own. But I am sure there are nameless, wonderful rewards awaiting me, if I can find an answer to high, pleasant walls, if I can find a walk to walk on my chubby, unsure legs. If I can negotiate the impossible, love awaits. With its endless motor, with its mysterious mixing of good-smelling ingredients. Yes, love is out there waiting for me to come to it.

Black

Notice how all the panes of colored glass are bordered in black. It forms a thin but strong encircling web holding all the designs in place. Sooty in its black density, it is impenetrable to both your and my eyes.

In this blackness rests all origins. In its murky negation the repose required for regeneration takes place. All potentiality resides in this darkness. All secrets—the scary and the wondrous—wait in this blackness.

My first encounter with the potent possibility of secret darkness happened in this way.

*   *   *

A young girl listens to a conversation in Spanish—words she doesn't understand. Her mother and a friend's voices meander through a leisurely *plática*—a rarity since the mother married and moved away.

The little girl's white leather shoes are shined every Sunday night by her father, who whistles at the task in a white T-shirt and khakis. He lines up two pairs of shoes for everyone in the family. One pair of school shoes; one pair for Church. He polishes each by first scraping an old toothbrush in a flat, round tin of paste polish. The crushed bristles reach into the crevice between the upper leather and the sole. Then he applies polish with a rag made from a soft sock. He buffs each shoe with a horsehair wooden brush.

The girl likes the garden where they are sitting adjacent to this lady's house. It is thriving—full of bushes and trees with mysterious, beautiful flowers. A mosaic of colored, chipped tile to walk on. Everything is miraculous on this Sunday afternoon in San Antonio, Texas.

The women enjoy talking. The little girl doesn't tire of being good. Just sitting in this garden, just being around this tiny, dark woman who paints pictures is a treat. The girl has never met a painter before. She has never before considered the magic that happens on canvas before the frame is set.

After a long time, the little girl needs a bathroom. The lady waves her inside the house. *¿Recuerdas donde está el baño?* The child doesn't understand or answer the foreign words. She remembers a tall, white, wooden door near the bedrooms.

The child isn't thinking about anything. She is too much in love with the patio—its colors and large plants. The happiness of a ruffled Sunday dress. New socks. She opens the door and walks in. At the end of the long narrow room is a man seated. He is the artist's husband of many years. His long-sleeved church shirt is off; his grey trousers around his ankles. There are no details, really. Only darkness. Incredible, palatable, sooty darkness. Masses of black crinkly hair embedded between his legs. His skin is dark too—richer than the little girl has ever seen except on black people.

The little girl quickly closes the door shutting out his face, turning from reflective to startled. She never wants to see such dark mystery again. She returns silent to the sun-filled patio. She will never tell anyone of this.

Gilt

If you glance away from the stained glass window, then back again, your eyes will be caught by the arcs of shining above the heads of the figures. These shimmering haloes represent all that we are meant to believe separates the divine from us. The iridescence of God's power and heavenly grace. The special favor of holiness. It is meant to beguile the eyes. Its glister is meant to encourage choosing a life-pattern like the lives of the figures frozen holy in the glass.

Sometimes the gilded grace appears in another fashion. This is my first memory of it.

*   *   *

It is a Saturday afternoon. Houston, Texas. A little girl sits in a two-toned green Oldsmobile with rocket ship tail lights. The car is parked next to an island of two pumps in a neighborhood filling station. Her father is inside the office paying for his gasoline. She glimpses the chaos of Tom's peanuts in a round glass-barreled vat. The waxy green of Dentler's potato chip bags. A black and oily floor—just like the hands and clothing of the men who work here.

When another car drives up, a different attendant walks out. He is young and has removed his shirt. Perhaps, for the sunshine and breeze. The small child on the passenger side of the green Olds has never seen a man's chest wholly naked. He saunters as if the slight wind is sidling against the tanned abundance of muscle. As he prepares to clean the front windshield, he jokes and laughs with the other driver. The girl hears him explain how fizzed-up Coca-Cola cleans windshields the best yet. He agitates the thick green glass bottle holding his own Coke, his thumb held against the opening. When he has it to his liking, he inverts the bottle and lets a stream spew out onto the windshield. Then he wipes it with slow and deliberate strokes.

The little girl is old enough to know that a woman's or girl's chest cannot be uncovered in daylight, in public. She feels such great longing inside her chest that she bypasses jealousy, bypasses envy. Instead, she becomes him. Becomes a young, handsome man alive in the palace of being male, being uncovered in the sun, of having so many options.

Blood-red

The color that next demands attention is a blood-red crimson. Here in the sunlight it is the color of melted rubies, the inside of a beating heart, or a flat icon in a deck of cards. The color that signifies life and signals death. A red gash streaming in the jungle—wet and dangerous. Slick. It gives unsure footing. To some, it gives heaving innards at its sight.

This color is my own unlived dream to be a warrior—a soldier fighting. My dreaming time of every childhood night for years will be filled with battle, uniforms, guns.

Sometimes the dream goes like this.

*   *   *

This is exactly how they told us it would be. Everything dirty, even me—unshaven for days, wearing the same stinking uniform. The entire squad's feet always hurting. I've never been this thin. I eat every time there's food. But my body doesn't care because I'm tired deep into the marrow of my bones. All of us are. Sick too, of fried Spam and powdered eggs served on square metal plates.

Do the folks back home understand? Naw. They never will. They don't have to. Only the civilians here comprehend living with death every moment. Some of them have been doing it for years 'cause Jerry invaded them and stuck around. Everyone in the States scrimps and saves, buys War Bonds. Every girl wants a soldier—some of them, three or four—to write to, to send cookies that arrive stale but smelling of vanilla and sweetness. I don't have a girl. That way I can dream about any girl without feeling like I'm betraying someone special.

Some of my buddies say, what's wrong? Don't you like girls? I say, sure. Sure, I like them plenty. Especially those with long legs and dark wavy hair.

Our corporal is a lot older than any of us. Maybe, twenty-eight or thirty. He says, Kid. Kid, you don't know what you're missing. Then he smiles and looks far off over my shoulder. My wife—my wife is a little piece of heaven, Kid.

What I won't say is, remember? Remember how they said you talk in your sleep after the War? You talk—maybe about things you did or saw. I can't have anyone around for that. Here, bivouacked in heaps on the ground after the same bloody work, it doesn't matter. But back home—what if I talk and don't know it?

Brown

Brown is the color of origin. Color of earth. Brown is the color that my family comes from in all our convoluted, known and unknown history of lineage across Texas and Mexico. Brown is the color of our skin. Skin of Apache. Skin of Comanche. Brown is the color of Mexico and Mexicans; brown the color of the good earth for crops.

This is the color of richness and complexity, tradition and loss. The color of pride in the many ancestors who gave us the blood in our veins. Brown is the color I am always looking for. My dream of it goes like this.

*　　*　　*

I am waiting for my husband to get home from work. I have already chopped celery, onion, bell pepper into the tiny chunks he likes in the meat's gravy. There will be plenty of garlic, oregano, and toasted comino seeds. He will eat well—scooping each bite with tortilla and swallowing deep draughts of water from the tall glass with yellow roses.

He is still the most handsome man I have ever seen. Even the guys at work kid him sometimes, saying he should've been an actor in the Mexican cinema during its heyday. What they are trying to say is that he looks like a lover, not a husband. This child in my belly will have our dark, rich skin and straight black hair.

When we met in high school, I thought, "No, not him. He's too good-looking. He'll be too much trouble." Then, we started walking home after his basketball practices. His hair combed back and wet from the shower. The scent of soap fresh— rising from everywhere on him. Neck, cheeks, arms. His eyes would light up and slowly I began to trust. He carried an ironed, white handkerchief in his back right pants pocket—just like my dad. None of the white girls wanted to date Mexican guys, not even ones as good-looking as him. So I began to give him parts of me. Fingertips, earlobes, arms, legs. Heart.

So, did he choose me or did I choose him? Even though we've been married for close to ten years I still wonder. He says it was my long hair— the sweet-smelling sheets of it blowing across his bare arms. He says it was destiny— our eyes the same dark pots of mystery, our skin the same mestizo. But I think my parents chose him. Not because they knew him or his family, but in a scarier, more holy way. They chose him by the way they trained me. By all the teaching from my mother and my *tías* about how you wear make-up every day even at the house, home alone. By how you cook hot meals every day—three times, with fresh tortillas at breakfast and dinner. How to clean a kitchen floor. How to iron every week on Friday afternoons before he gets home. Elsewhere, I learned to wear white lace against my skin, or red only. Nightgowns that force cleavage. How to warm his blood.

I let him think he chose me all those years ago. After all, the man's place is to make decisions, to take care of his woman. To place family first in his life. But I know my mother created me—unknowingly—to be with no one but him.

*   *   *

He steps through the front door. I loosen the knot of my apron and ready my heart. Each evening I hug him when he gets home and is just inside the door.

His hair is combed away from his face. He has already loosened the knot of his tie and tugged it to one side. The tortilla dough is resting in small, white rounds on the board. He pushes me into the bedroom while kissing one ear. Already lost in the faint scent of cologne below his rough cheek, I tug at his belt and buckle.

I try to think for a second if all the burners are off on the stove. I settle into the familiarity of his desire, this large belly not stopping either one of us. I know what I will teach my child and I know what my child is already learning.

Vegetation

Step closer. Lift up your hand. Place your fingertips on the green whorl of trees in the distance, off to the side. It feels cold and smooth, doesn't it? Close your eyes and imagine yourself below the green, leafy canopy in a forest. Listen for the hum of insects and the slight breeze through the leaves.

It is safe in this forest. No marauders; no encounters with evil cloaked in spun sugar and gingerbread. No one to woo danger into the tiers of leafy green. It is this safety, this peacefulness that most people seek. Not me. The many-hued leaves and dank undergrowth of rot have always called me into a dream of danger. A dream of warfare. If I'd been a boy, I would've gone to 'Nam. I was the right age; the right race. This is my dream of what I missed, what I still could do.

Keep your hand steady on the glass colored like swirling leaves while you look. Understand, if you can, the flight into danger, the desire for battle.

*   *   *

Ripe, fat, mango moon. You don't look that way at home. Back there you're white and cold. Dimpled in grey. I used to watch you on late nights at the ball field or from an early duck blind. Here you watch us with that yellowish underbelly. Waiting.

Let me tell you something. Fresh meat. That's all we are. The jungle waiting to absorb us into its thousand-year ooze of rot. That smell has it all—dead animals, dead trees, dead us, all the exfoliating chemicals sprayed from the big choppers. That smell never leaves you. Even on R&R after genuine hot showers and clean clothes. Cologne, After-Shave—forget it. They don't help. The smell gets so far into your skin and hair, under your fingernails, in between your toes, that it never goes away.

If you get lucky enough once you're killed, they'll be able to find all your parts and bag you up. Then they'll load you into a chopper—with or without a bag. Maybe you'll be lucky enough to have some other poor grunt close your eyes before he bags you up. Maybe not. Me— I'd hate to have to stare at the slick, black underside of heavy-duty plastic the whole trip outta here. I want some rest before my funeral 'cause we don't get no rest here. Maybe you or me getting blown up will make the five o'clock news, so the people back home can watch. You know they watch us getting killed every night on T.V., don't you? We're fucking entertainment to them.

Girls!? The girls here are scary. They don't even look like real girls. They're miniatures. You can't trust them. They all work for Charlie. Yeah—death in high-heel sandals. I wouldn't go to one. I bet even their cunts are booby-trapped, like everything else here. Can you imagine? Can you fucking imagine? Boom!

They want us to walk down that trail tonight. Condition Red and they want us to go out? Crazy desk jockeys! Show me one guy with brass who knows what it's really like out here and I'll shoot my brains out myself. Yeah . . . Boom! Boom!

Don't eat before you go out. It's bad luck. Besides you don't want all that food gushing through and up your insides when you're walking the jungle. Charlie can hear things we can't. Even the jungle itself hears stuff. You'll be walking along and then suddenly for no reason, everything stops the noise it was making—birds, bugs, animals. Everything goes crazy silent. Fresh meat for Charlie. Boom!

Sometimes I can dream. Although, you know that you can't close your eyes when you sleep here, don't you? Yeah, keep your peepers open, man. You got to be able to see everything all the time. You may get killed anyway, but at least you'll see it coming. You'll get an up close visual—you'll see yourself become Fresh Meat. Boom!

When I dream, I dream about some kind of incredible American girl. She's got long legs from hours of tennis and volleyball in the sun. She's got a smile as big as heaven. She's wearing starched and ironed, baby-blue shorts and a midriff top. Every solid inch of her showboat legs and ribs will be tanned to a golden, honey-brown. We'll be talking – not about the War. Not about anything from 'Nam. Maybe, I'll get to hug her. Maybe I'll get to hold her hand. I'll be cleaned up real good. Hey—I'll take a hot shower for four hours before I touch her. Her hair will be a long cascade of brown, smelling of shampoo and long hours of slow brushing. I got four sisters, so I know about brushing. And when I hug her, when I bury my whole face in the cave of neck and hair and earlobe, her soap scent – clean, God Almighty – sweet and clean, will go so deep inside every pore of me that I'll never smell this jungle again. Never smell rotting death again. Never be here in my dreams again.

The Blue Ribbon

A blue ribbon—its outlines embroidered in uniform, tiny stitches—floats across the white expanse of a starched pillowcase. The pillow next to it has been stitched in the same design but its ribbon is scarlet. A clear, bright, happy color that implies good, hot food on the dinner table served promptly at six every evening. A small, white and tan dog barks outside the dinner table's room. Daddy has just gotten home.

*   *   *

I remember learning to embroider. The blue, hazy lines of a design ironed by mom on new cloth from a tissue paper transfer. Did she or I choose that first design? I don't remember. But since I was only five or six year old, she must've chosen.

The design is transferred onto a large cotton square. It will be a dishcloth when I am done with it. There is a breakfast tray with handles. It holds a waffle iron I will do in grey thread I fancy looks silver; a small cream pitcher and sugar bowl I will do in two shades of green. Sunday morning hospitality captured in graceful curves and the ample promise of steaming food.

Mother instructs me how to thread a needle. How to begin a line, so there won't be a knot on the reverse side of the towel. I learn that embroiders are judged by both sides of their work.

It is hard to keep the stitches regular. My young fingers and mind can't quite catch hold of the relationship between the tension of the thread and a stitch's outcome. Even harder is remembering to pick up the cloth to peek at its underside after each stitch is done. Already I have learned that the ugly tangle of a knot may be concealed by a smooth, even stitch up top.

Mother is patient; I grow tired. For today, I've started learning a grown-up skill. One of the array of mysteries I see even in our calm, orderly household.

My head is filled with combinations of threads, stitches, and designs. I glory in the planning. The anticipation of choosing to make beautiful designs in bright colors for the kitchen and bathroom—just as my mother and grandmother have done for years—is overwhelming. I've just entered into a new universe—one that can be gained by planning and hard work. One in which the results are beauty. Surely, this comprises being an adult.

*   *   *

Many years after mother taught me to embroider and quite some time after I knew by heart her stories of all the women at the farm sitting evenings by the radio listening to World War II for news of battles their husbands, sons, brothers, cousins, friends were fighting, she told me her secret. She said that she had always disliked embroidering. How all the details made her nervous. How she didn't find it relaxing; had never found it relaxing. Hated sewing.

French knot. Cross-stitch. Lazy daisy. Satin stitch. Outline stitch.

I pick up a sharp needle. Lick the end of the thread. Choose a bright color. Puncture the close-woven cotton. Create flowers to lie in.

The Looking

You now possess our secrets, our dreams, our holiest beliefs. You have looked through each facet of the stained-glass window. You have seen how the colors sometimes distort what is on the other side; you have seen how they may make what is outside more beautiful. You know what pierces each of us. Perhaps, you see glimmers of the healing.

Let go of my hand. Look at the world on the other side of the window alone. Now, you are ready to see and understand what happened through the lens of what we believed, what we yearned for, what we couldn't or didn't choose.

SECTION TWO

Costume Jewelry

Gosh, I loved the colors.
Each facet a story
called forth
from light
into the shimmer
of Mom's bracelets, matching
earrings, single-strand necklaces.

A simpler world
then? Short-haired men
glad to be back alive
from European and Pacific
Theaters. Young wives
wearing scarlet lipstick
in modest evening gowns.

Those night club couples
happy just to dance
in the arms
of a thin sweetheart
after years of airmail
APO stationery and scanning
lists of dead in newspapers.

The faceted loops
and colorful abundance
of victory. Its

promised
endless prosperity.

On South Main

Beyond the straw-hatted ponies
for hire, colorful
arcing neon lit
my imagination.

A huge blue-white crab
sat on one roof, lit claws raised
into sky. His domain a fresh Gulf
seafood restaurant.

Parallel ribbons
of tubed light for Princess
hamburgers brought
by smiling, lipsticked girls,

beautiful in short, cowgirl skirts,
tasseled white boots. Their
Western fringe jerking
a happy dance of eating

to come, orders hot
off the large grill
in back. All guarded
by Pegasus'

red silhouette
high downtown.

His unfailing wings lifted
into the black rectangle
of night. My reclining, fulsome vision
through our car's back window

driving home.

Pot of Rouge

Charles of the Ritz, opaque
black pot storing red
possibilities. White-lidded
receptacle sitting on mom's vanity.
Depository of all my ill-formed dreams.

Once at age three I unscrewed
the top, imbedded my fingers
into luscious, blue-red creaminess.
Smeared it on my lips, cheeks,
peering into the big round mirror.

Sincere transformation. Then, I rubbed
thick redness into white net curtains
billowed out by heavy summer breeze
like a bridal veil, felt the push
of my womanhood beckoning

toward some unknown.

The Donut Hole

It's a small shack, a tiny
rectangular building covered
in forest-green wood siding,
beige trim. Screened front door
centered. A proud sign in a shell lot.

Fresh donuts lined up
on wooden racks, angled
downward to show off
glazed abundance, an
orderly decadent array.

Hot, light dough. Jelly-
filled—tangy lemon, grape,
or a sweet dark red. Plain
unglazed for dunking—even
some with handles!

The miracle greater than
just-made donuts—a square,
sliding, screened-in window
in the side of the building
for drive-up customers.

The lady slides up the screen,
cocks her ear to the order,
fills a brown paper bag, takes
coins or bills. Punches the register.

As much as I want my donut,
even more I want to stay, watching
the lady lean against the window's
small ledge, listen to the outside,

dispense juicy happiness, smells,
good grease, innocent pleasure
through the wondrous sliding
of that small, wood-framed,
newly-screened window.

I slip one hand into Dad's khaki pocket,
stumbling over my feet on the way
out, still trying to look, to catch
it all until the next sweet time.

Being Five

I wonder at the brilliant blue
hair of a colored lady I see
on Saturday's grocery outing. At
great risk of a stern shoulder pull
from my mother, I stare—
loving the iridescent, cobalt blue,
carefully-curled hairstyle. Her
deep black skin, so smooth
and shining. I want my hair
to be the same some day,
when I don't have to skip
at my mother's side
in seersucker plaid shorts,
tanned legs, knock-knees.
Transparent with unbidden longing.

Chow Dog

Black chow's purple
tongue. We cringe
glimpsing it. We
don't believe
the hurricane fence
can hold him.

Not when he lunges,
spit flying, teeth bared,
shiny white and sharp. When
he's resting under the shade
tree, we shove against
the fence, giggling.

Into the chain links
he hurls himself, doesn't
slow or stop. He hates
us, wants to eat us,
that scaly tongue savoring
our eyeballs and flimsy throats.

We race away and scream,
scooters careening. When
the next-door lady comes
home from work, she opens
the louvered back-porch slats
and coos, "Nice doggie."

Aunt Aurora

She was the only
wife married into either side
of our dark Mexican family
with real blonde hair, yellow-green

eyes. To me she was
the leggy calendar girl above the footed
tub at the farm. An easy smile
above ideal paper waist, full chest,

bright curls. She spoke a smiling Spanish
like all the adults when we
visited the farm. The women
gabbing in the rotating breeze

of a heavy-footed Admiral fan,
twirling flour-sack towels
in a working flurry of pastel designs
and crocheted lace. Her husband,

my uncle—always the most
handsome. Full lips, parted
above a swagger
of body-building muscle. The

only one whose tongue
took pleasure in cutting sarcasm
and endless, logical debates. Once
I saw him slit open a steer's

belly—just butchered and still
warm. The methodical pull
of whitish intestines. It was

what he loved—a quick stab,

the ripping apart from a
sturdy perch, knife in hand.

Magic

Flowing garments, long hair,
or streaming veils. The list—
endless. Superman winning
all in his cape. Ben-Hur,
red cloak streaming behind his chariot.
Zorro, dressed in midnight, smiling.

Even the Blessed Virgin Mary's
sky-blue veil encompassed
the globe. Our nuns standing
in the playground, a blossom
opened at a throat by a breeze
quickly put to order, linen fluttering.

Mary Magdalene with her shimmering
hair drying the exposed feet of Jesus.
The black-and-white gypsy women
dancing against firelight
to unwritten music, urgent clapping hands.
Their coin necklaces bouncing against the sway.

My hair was dismally short
and frizzled near the edges. Yet
once—once I twirled
in the backyard alone.
Two panels of discarded, white net
curtains bobby-pinned to the part
at the center of my head.

My arms extended, fingers
combing the breeze, I spun
into circles leading the pretend
veil of hair into its own
floating transit. Yes, it was
magic. I remember exactly
how it felt. Yes.

Glow

From my twin bed
every night
I saw
a round, red ember
signaling
Dad's last cigarette.

In the total
fairy-tale darkness
I watched
that band—
like his wedding ring—
burn brighter

during inhales. Then
recede
to a dullness. As
long as I saw
the lucent redness
I knew

it was safe
to sleep. Daddy's
reassuring beacon
before
turbulent dreams
to come.

Fish To Catch

There's a small, black lake
next to Hermann Zoo. At
night, thickened roars of lions
tumble out low, bricked walls
through nearby clean streets.

We're here to fish
with other dads
or lone black men
or women. Always at night
in the summer without mom.

I have my own dark green,
marbled tackle box. My own
small, irregular steel weights,
many sizes of hooks, a
cork or two with a pin sticking

up through the top. Daddy
holds up a cardboard tube
of thin, black hooks—
one-pronged, delicate.
He says, "These will catch

us some fish here!" His
eyes sparkle green. He
shows me where to cast. We
sit on the pier beneath tall
lamp posts fishing. It's important

to know how to set the hook. Reel
in slowly. Guide the net. Don't
hurt the fish's mouth. Throw

it back for next time. Wait silent
above lapping black water.

Go home
full of small successes.

Happiness

Loosie and Toosie arrived
in a brown paper bag with cutouts
one Easter morning—a surprise
to me from Daddy and Mom.

The household rearranged
itself inside and out
accommodating two tiny, yellow puffs
I had named in rhymes.

Loosie and Toosie pureed
the dog's food in his ceramic bowl
before he got to it. They walked into
Mom's orderly garage and shat.

They were scared of the billowing
washday sheets on the line, but
squawked and circled Blackie,
the outdoor cat, in St. Augustine grass.

They explored every hole
in the chain link fence
patrolling for pill bugs,
juicy slugs, and freedom.

One summer before we drove
to Washington, D.C., my parents told me
no one could feed my ducks during vacation.
Loosie and Toosie had to go away.

We could drop them off
at the lake across
from the Zoo. With so many

other ducks, they'd be happy.

Daddy bought two expandable plastic rings
at the hardware store—light
blue, pale green. By now their
feet were large, yellow, thick.

Daddy put them in a cardboard box.
Silent, he and I drove that evening
to let them go near the small black lake.

When we returned from vacation,
Daddy and I went to visit them, picking
out pale color against mud, white flip
of tail feathers. I wanted to know if
they were happy. Daddy said *yes*.

Yes. I'm sure. But, I couldn't tell.

I rode home on my side
of the wide front seat
full of that first question
and of all the many uncertain answers.

Return

Thick, maroon blood
across our light-green Oldsmobile's
trunk, rear bumper, dripping in the driveway.
Daddy's home from deer hunting. One
strapped down, tongue lolling. Its

liquid eyes still open. My
first time seeing death
unshuttered, unblinking, leaking
heavily across smooth metal. Sweet
smell of pocket-flask bourbon.

Daddy and the other hunter
haven't shaved in days.
Mom says they smell
"ripe." Their eyes rimmed in thin,
red mucous. Voices excited.

The tail is white. Hide,
short and brownish. Hooves
black, legs numbed. *We're
going to the meat place.
Do you want to come along?*

I can't ride in a car
that near a carcass,
so I wait in the spic-and-span
kitchen, grey-tiled counter top.

Dinner fragrant.

Bill William's Fried Chicken

Dining out on a Sunday
after late Mass
we sit at a round table.
Plate glass surrounds
us. Suits and ties, dark
mid-calf dresses under straw
hats for the ladies. Shoes
fresh with polish. The waitresses

sporting pale-blonde buns
under no-nonsense hair nets, and lozenge-
shaped little aprons against white.
Each stainless fork, knife, coffee
spoon is shiny and brand-new.
White sugar crystallizing in a glass
tower only Daddy gets to use.
Creamery milk for me.

Dad closes his menu; he always
orders the same thing. Mom and I look
longer. We always order the same thing
too but revel in the reckless pretend.

          *   *   *

Honey on the table longing
for the heat. Honey waiting
for dripping, buttery biscuits.
Coiled splurge lacing into warmth.

          *   *   *

The food comes!

Perfection parading
as crisp fried chicken,
mashed potatoes, brown
gravy, biscuits we want
to die in. Butter melting
in gold rivulets I pursue
with eager tongue.

The thick sugar ooze
of honey snuggles into butter.
Over and over each of us picks up
the smooth glass jar, slides
the top backwards and pours
tanned honey
through the small metal window
onto a biscuit.

We don't even eat dessert. Driving
home with all the windows
down, easing out of girdle
and garter belt, or double-Windsored
polka-dot tie, or tight patent
leather shoes is enough
richness, enough reward.

Surf Fishing

Daddy taught me—warm
Gulf tugging through long pants
and up our shirted chests.
Bait bucket
on a leader
of white rope.

Always too much sand
to see into the water. But
once in a while
a mouth or claws
came for our legs, feet, toes.

Mostly, we pulled up perch.
Less than pan-sized
got thrown back. White flesh,
rainbowed scales, dark
unwavering eyes.

Mom collected driftwood, built
a fire. Fried our catch in heavy
cast-iron, grease sputtering.
Starbursts of cornmeal,
pepper and salt,
in kerosene lantern light.

We slept leeward
of our car but awoke
with salty grit everywhere. All
for the love of surf rolling in,
white crests against warm blackness,
eerie trickles of wind.

Haunt

We girls sang Mass;
boys were altar boys.
Every morning before school
single file, silent,
hands folded in prayer
we marched into the Church.

Once during Mass
a flying shape—quick and small—
darted in a window. It was dark.
I think, scared. It circled
the glittering altar with its candles
then flew up into our choir loft.

We were in the middle
of a song. Sister pumping the organ
with tiny feet in laced black leather
against wood. It landed
on one girl's beanie. Too disciplined
to react, I chanted memorized Latin staring

only at the hummingbird. Then
Roseanne, the tall girl with glasses, reached,
placed her hand over the emerald bird's flutter,
caught it. Trapped, it squealed
once. She took it outside, down
the stairs, let it go. I still hear it.

Muffled in her hand. Hurt.
Surprised, and struggling.

Seguin

What did she
do in long summer
afternoons standing
inside the small,
square window

three houses over
from our house? Her
son faint
and washed out
in my memory

except for stiff,
blonde crew cut, a
small boy's
thin shoulders,
tanned elbows and knees.

Their house a white
wood shingle with no
front sidewalk. No
husband we knew of
in our church or

at the nearby grocery.
Somehow I heard
she was from Seguin.
A place I didn't
know, a place I

forever linked
with a thin woman's
tall shadow in a house

I never entered. The flat
plane of empty, the troubled

call for home. A
starched white blouse
behind a high screened window
over an empty kitchen sink.

The Gift

Mom teaches school
in an old white building
massive in mystery—
connecting passageways,
graceful arches, the only
basement in my childhood.

One other teacher—a lady—
is horribly short. *A dwarf,*
mother whispers to me at home.
My mother wants to be a decent
friend. The lady visits our house.
She has wavy blonde hair, thickened legs.

At Christmas she gives
my mom a small present.
The wrapping reveals a square,
white box holding a round
powder puff. A cloud of downy
peach too delicate for touch.

The yielding softness beckons—ready,
impractical. My mother explains
that teacher wants friends,
is lonely, gives expensive gifts
ordinary people can't use.

When I see that small teacher
in my mind now, I want to ask
impossible questions. How to find truth
in a craven world, how to look
for tenderness and never give up.

Baycliff

Our next door neighbors,
the Witts, rent a cabin
each weekend for the whole
summer, hauling their sleek
boat full of large, red ice-chests.

We go only a few times
each season. Before, Dad
cleans his fishing gear; I clean
mine. Mom packs condiments
in small glass jars
with screw top lids.

Each cabin has square Melamine
plates, frying pans, precarious
gas burners, moist salt, black pepper,
splintery toothpicks
in an empty Tabasco jar.

We bring the rest—eggs,
bacon, cornmeal, white bread,
pump-spray Off. Small canned Vienna
sausages like chubby toes. Everywhere
a shrimpy saltiness in each inhale.

In the mornings, Dad and I
walk a shell path
to the pier. We scout
for the numbered fiberglass boat
he's rented. Short pier creaking.

We load fishing poles, tackle
boxes, a squat dented water cooler.

The sputtering outboard purrs
into the tepid Gulf. Small
bait-well shrimp swimming backwards.

We come back before dark.
Reddened cheeks and legs. The
sun's sparkle on waves caught
inside our skins. Even later, asleep—
I'm hot, so thoroughly cooked.

At night the women fry the fish;
the men drink cold beers. Mosquitoes'
delicate landings on oiled, tanned limbs.
Stories becomes bigger stories, the
men's eyes go bloodshot. More Off.

We sleep on screened-in porches
in soft humid beds covered with light
blue and green plaid bedspreads.
Rotating fans for breeze. When I
close my eyes, I feel the boat's rocking

still.

Joe Angel

It must've been gutters
he came to sell
to Mom and Dad. Me,
not old or pretty enough
to matter to a stranger. But

those were earlier times
when even a salesman
got invited to lunch
or early dinner with
a big glass of cold

milk. I'd never seen
or dreamt a man
so delicately handsome.
Curls roiling off
his forehead above jade eyes.

He seemed to enjoy
our food and my parents'
conversation. I kept
silent—not needing
to talk, just admiring

his prettiness, better than a girl's.

We bought his gutters;
signed a contract. After
he left, Mom pointed
to his name on the papers.
Joe Angel. She and I

agreed—he was that utterly

beautiful. Like a gold-tipped angel
in church. Some time later mom told me
he had killed himself. I
wanted to know why

and I still do. When I search
my memory of his polite smiles
during dinner or the way he
looked at us, I can't find
answers. Light pink in his

cheeks. An unbuttoned sports coat.
A slender leather belt.
Because he ate and visited
with us, we considered him
a friend. How could he kill

himself? I see his smooth face
as Daddy, he and I walk
in the backyard. They are
talking gutters, looking overhead,
and I am admiring the perfect

symmetry of a beautiful stranger.
We circle the garage,
whose painted lumber houses
the thick, green glass
of empty 7-Up bottles,

Daddy's decoys in burlap,
waiting for cold winter ponds
and the high, wild call
in leaden skies. Our small dog's
bed. None of it enough

to keep any of us
alive.

The Claiming

Sometime before I turned
teen, my mother gave me
Mitzi, a grown-up doll
like Barbie but with brown
eyes—a pony-tailed brunette.

There were outfits galore
but no corresponding dark-headed
Ken doll. I didn't need one.
My imagination supplying boys—
all intrigue, adventure, good looks.

Mitzi's curves were hard
plastic and uncolored. Nothing
realistic. No dark, sensitive
nipples or wrinkled, ripe gash
mysterious between her legs. No tears.

Brown like me. I wanted
to paint her womanliness. I
took nail polish, gave her
nipples. Pubic hair. Forever
clear, neon-orange markers.

Forever scared Mom would see,
know the signs
of my own curiosity
my own darkness,
my own future.

Realization

How I hated going
to their three-story,
white house every morning
before seventh grade. The
only car pool with other Catholic
kids close by.

They were an Irish family.
Ghostly pale and mostly blonde,
freckled. The trim, quiet dad
a career doctor in a famous program.
Crusted sleep rimming his pale eyes
each morning. Ten kids; one a year.

Very early my parents dropped me
off in a muddy side yard.
Sitting in a dark downstairs den,
I'd study. Each child drifting
by on the way to burnt toast
and milk that stayed out to sour.

Pat, the boy one year older
than me, walking barefoot
on dirty winter floors. The next
to youngest baby boy
losing stained diapers
down chubby legs.

Their immense black maid
maneuvering through the uproar
and clatter of ten children,
one a year. Good Catholics.
They filled Sunday's church pew—

a long row of groomed silence and gilt-edged

missals. The mom's dark, lank hair
always pulled off her face. She
smiled a lot. Often the hollows
below her eyes were full of blood,
purple and latent under fragile skin.
She said it was anemia. She said it
often. So many babies had made her
anemic. So many years later
sitting in a classroom
it hits me—
she had black eyes;
he was beating her.

Ten kids; one a year.
Pale eyelashes; delicate skin.

Delivery

No man other
than family
came in
through the kitchen.

Until we hired
a milkman when I
was thirteen. Oh, we
were always up and dressed

on Saturday mornings

and he always knocked
loudly before he brought
in a sea of white, starched
uniform, hat. The cold milk

in square glass gallons.

Pretty blue eyes that
always tried
too hard not to look
at Mom in a cotton house dress.

I didn't trust him.

Felt a violation in his
every cushioned, careful step
on our polished linoleum. Hated
that he put milk in the fridge

himself, that he saw rectangular
glass containers holding

our next delicious meal. Prepared
promises, savory treasures he had

no right to see.

Visiting

Sharp rocks jumped
at our car's belly,
driving unpaved streets
to Laredo relatives. The
languages I didn't speak—
older girl cousins trilling
Spanish, dressing
for skinny, black-haired boys
in blue suits
while I
sat with the adults
at Formica tables,
listening.

Harmony Wedding Chapel

On the Galveston freeway's feeder
there's a white cottage
trimmed in unreal, dark blue.
Who wouldn't marry
in a church with a priest? Who

would hire a place like this
to wear the loveliest white gown
in your life? To be claimed
by handsome and bound
in gold rings stronger than death?

Driving south to the sea's claim,
I don't think my front-seat parents
ever saw it. From the sleek, two-toned Olds'
upholstered perch I imagined
a white filigreed magic inside

precious as spun sugar rosebuds.
One first cousin married there—quickly—
to a tall, pale *gringo*. She's the one
who doesn't like me so much now
because her younger brother

once grabbed me in the kitchen
at a family barbeque. She's married now
to another tall white guy. Does she
ever remember a Saturday
afternoon when her black eyes

flashed above a white bodice
sewn of tiny sparkling beads, and
a younger me felt
ashamed for a girl-cousin
who couldn't go to a priest?

Charlie

May 1969

He found me in my first year
of college before summer
break. He was a cheerleader,
a heart-throb senior. Not
too many guys liked him.

He drank Johnnie Walker
Black like some Yankee,
disdaining sour mash, marijuana,
acid. He hailed from Amarillo;
said he craved my cherry's taste.

One night we met a group
of his friends at a strip joint
off a back road. I couldn't believe
the huge bobbing breasts
above acrobatic bodies.

One dancer inserted one breast
inside a customer's beer mug
then jiggled his beer to a foam.
Everyone clapped but me, too
engrossed figuring out the foment,

the logic, the smells, so much
womanhood, so different from mine.
At break the loudspeakers requested
volunteers to dance on a small table
up front, lower than the real stage.

The door hostess pranced up, stiff
hair brushing her sagging face. A

prim grey dress, sleeveless. Black heels,
no hose. Fully clothed she danced
on the sturdy, round, wooden table,

ricocheting her pelvis
into each hard bass note.
The ending flourish
a deep bend that let us
see the backs of her legs

sinewy into opaque black panties.
No signs of aging there. They
asked again, "Volunteers?"
My date urged me on, cigar bobbing
as he winked and clapped. I knew

it'd turn him on, knew it'd
make him proud—my slim, flawless
legs. Knew my short skirt showed
them off real good. Almost
stood up; almost decided

to dance for strangers. But I
mistrusted the limelight, the cheap
wooden stage. Had always mistrusted
his undisguised desire, his insistent
prodding. Over the summer

he dropped me. But I never forgot
him or the call of his brand of danger.

Atlanta 1969

The first place foreign
I went was to Atlanta,
Georgia. Blazing hot, red
clay, June wedding. First-year
college friends marrying wealth

to wealth near tall pines. My
airport reception from a huge cop
as I jaywalked in tight,
egg-yolk yellow rayon,
mini-skirted dress and matching shoes,

"We don't do that here,
young lady." The hosting parents
paired me up with the
seventeen year old brother
of the dark-haired groom. Younger

brother had white-gold hair.
A surfer's tan. Serious pale-blue eyes.
Younger brother knew all the battles
of the Civil War by heart. He
smiled and proffered his arm in Church

and the rest of the weekend
recited battles to me—move by move. Slowly.
I ate my first bite of Baked Alaska. Sat
up late on banquettes in a real French
restaurant. Thought a blonde boy

handsome. My first taste of strange.

Question

I stand in a Church dressing room full
of deliberate wooden ornamentation.
My girlfriend wears a flowing, white satin
gown. She met the groom at eighth-grade
Science Camp; they plan to be doctors. He's already
at the altar, stiff and waiting in cut-away tux.

A small surprise gift arrives
from her groom. She
opens the box, lifts a long strand
of graduated pearls. The note
says he adores her. The pearls
are third generation family.

She considers their length
against her dress's neckline. She
looks aggravated—they're too long.
White thread is found; adjustments
made. She calls for her bouquet;
we scurry. How does she

take it all for granted? Displeased
porcelain skin between dark eyebrows.
Sweetheart neckline. Slender waist.

Walking Home

I know who and what
will be there
when I arrive.

Mom chopping for dinner.
Attic fan cooling. Small
white dog, tail furled, barking.

Daddy will come home.
At dinner I'll drink two glasses
of ice-cold milk. We'll talk.

I'll fall asleep beneath saints'
smiles after homework,
dishwashing, praying on knees.

*   *   *

I cannot go back. Can you?
Can you walk home? Everyone
dead or simply grown up.

*   *   *

Remember each detail, its beauty.
Survive the memory, its nearness.

Walk yourself home, then back here again.